the music glee
the showstoppers
volume 3

Series Artwork, Fox Trademarks and Logos
TM and © 2010 Twentieth Century Fox Film Corporation.
All Rights Reserved.

ISBN 978-1-4234-9665-6

HAL•LEONARD®
CORPORATION

7777 W. BLUEMOUND RD. P.O. BOX 13819 MILWAUKEE, WI 53213

Visit Hal Leonard Online at
www.halleonard.com

BAD ROMANCE

Words and Music by STEFANI GERMANOTTA
and NADIR KHAYAT

Rah, rah, ah, ah, ah. __ Ro - ma, ro - ma, ma. __ Ga - Ga, ooh - la - la, __

want your bad ro - mance. { I want your ug - ly, I want your dis - ease. __
{ I want your hor - ror, I want your de - sign __

I want your ev - 'ry - thing as long as it's free. __ I want your love.}
'cause you're a crim - i - nal as long as you're mine. __ I want your love.}

Love, love, love, I want your love.

I want your dra-ma, the touch of your _ hand, hey.
I want your psy-cho, your ver-ti-go _ shtick, hey.
I want your leath-er-stud-ded
While you in my rear win-dow,

kiss in the sand. _ I want your love.
ba-by is sick. _ I want your love.
Love, love, love, I want your

love, love, love, I want your love.
You know that I want you

Am

and you know that I need you. I want it bad, bad ro-mance. _

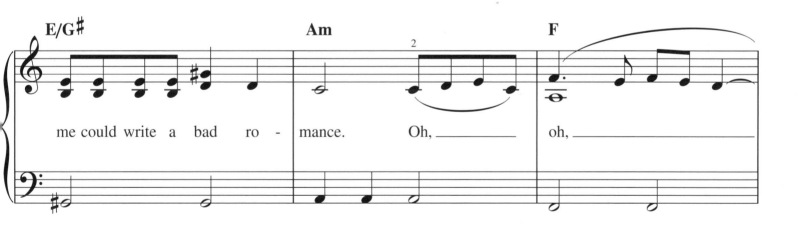

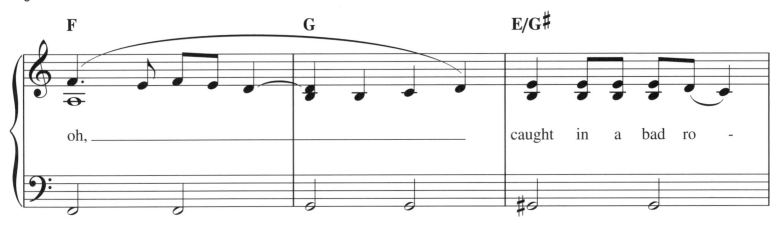

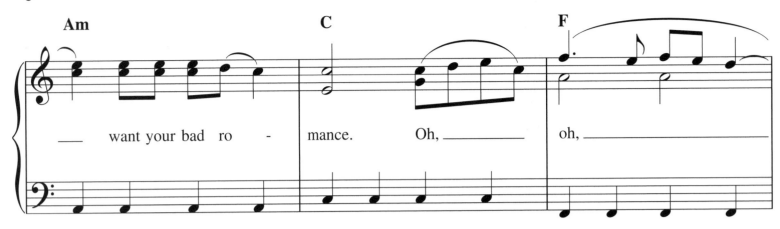

BEAUTIFUL

Words and Music by
LINDA PERRY

Moderately slow

mf *Whispered: Don't look at me.*

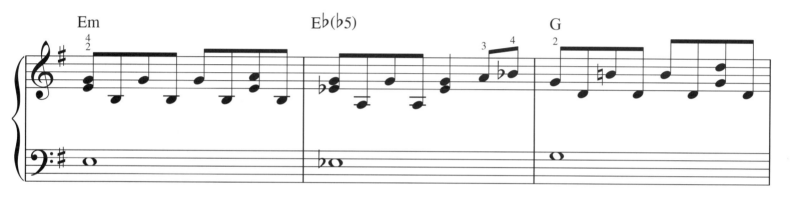

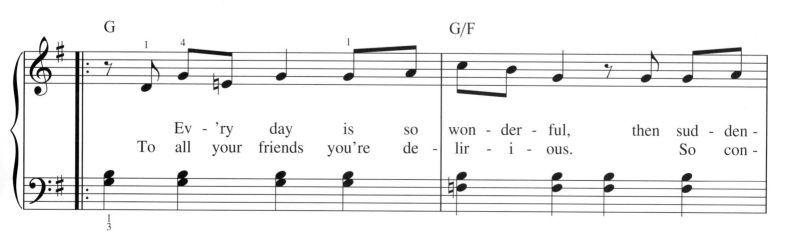

Ev - 'ry day is so won - der - ful, then sud - den -
To all your friends you're de - lir - i - ous. So con -

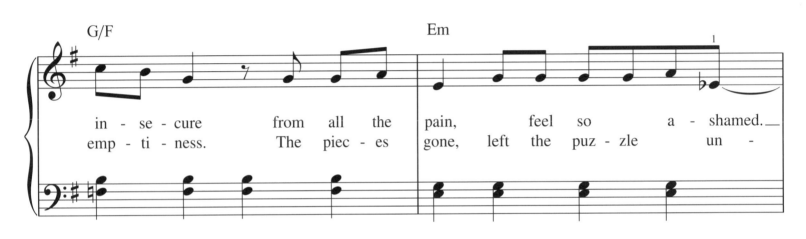

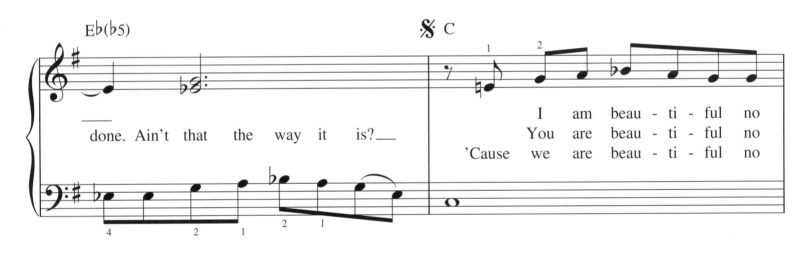

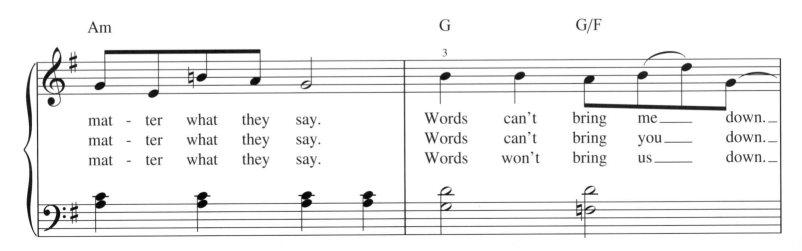

Em   C   Am

I am beau - ti - ful in ev -'ry sin - gle way.   Yes,
You are beau - ti - ful in ev -'ry sin - gle way.   Yes,
We are beau - ti - ful in ev -'ry sin - gle way.   Yes,

G   G/F   Em

words can't bring me____ down,____ ____   oh no._____
words can't bring you____ down,____   oh no._____
words won't bring us____ down,____   oh no._____

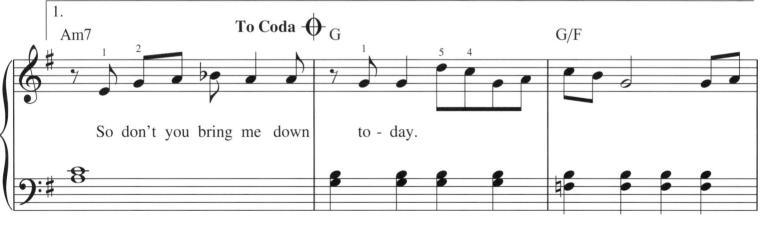

1.
Am7   **To Coda** G   G/F

So don't you bring me down   to - day.

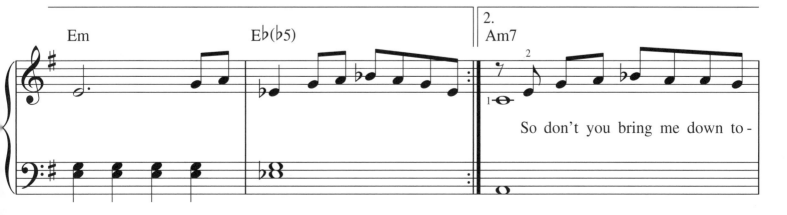

Em   Eb(b5)   2.
                                 Am7

So don't you bring me down to -

day. No mat - ter what we do. No mat - ter what we

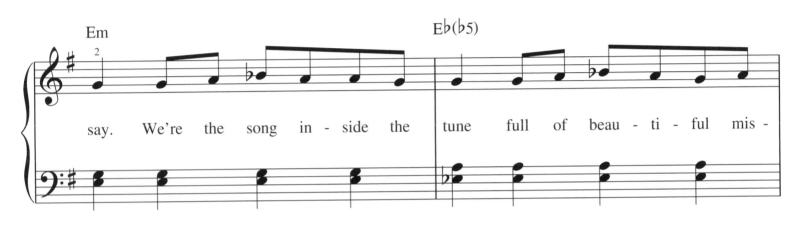

say. We're the song in - side the tune full of beau - ti - ful mis -

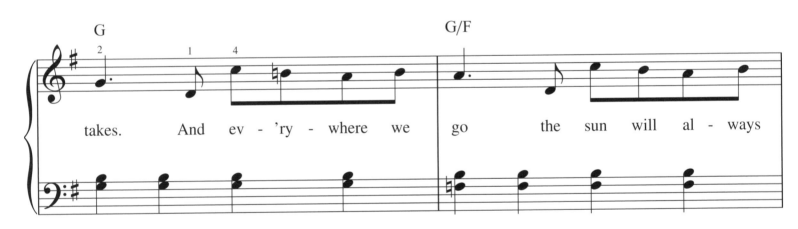

takes. And ev - 'ry - where we go the sun will al - ways

D.S. al Coda
(take 1st ending)

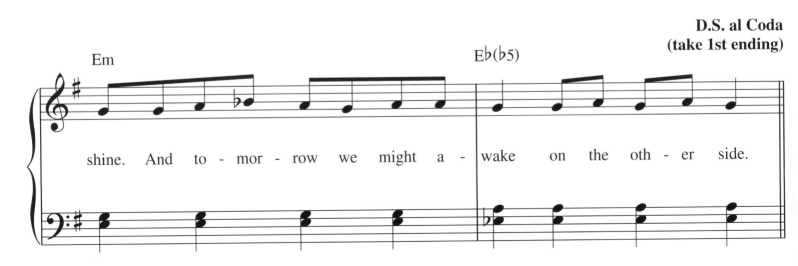

shine. And to - mor - row we might a - wake on the oth - er side.

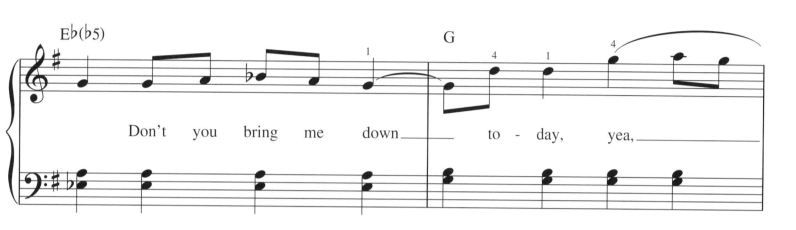

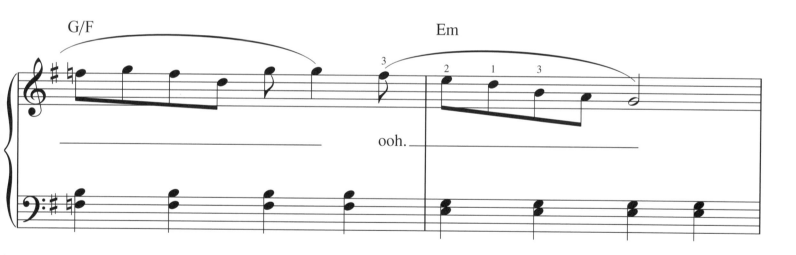

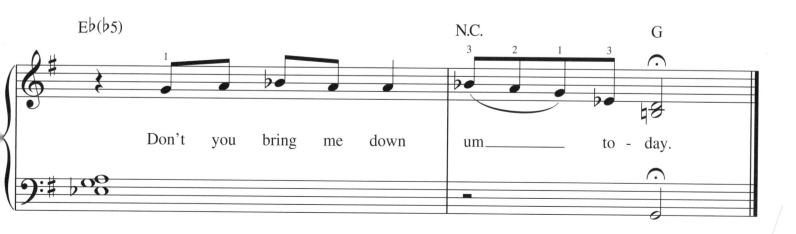

DREAM ON

Words and Music by
STEVEN TYLER

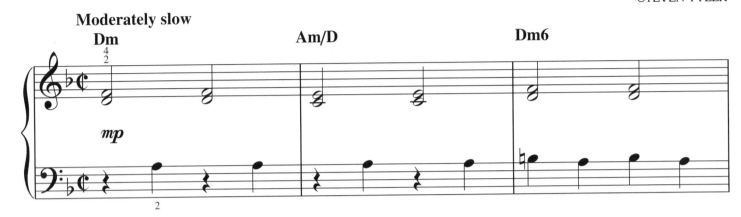

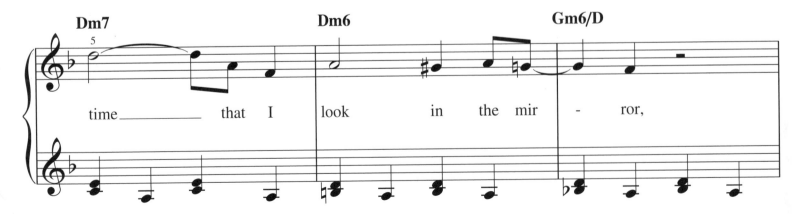

time_____ that I look in the mir - ror,

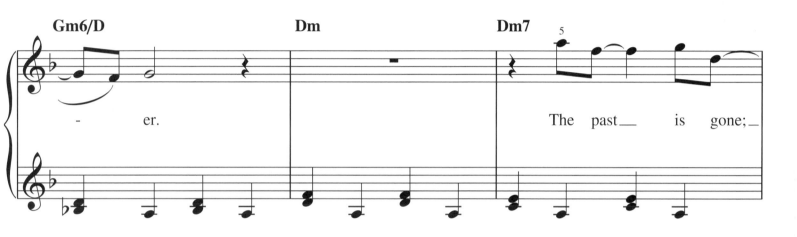

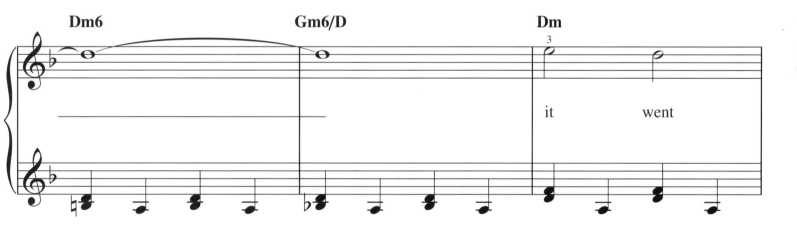

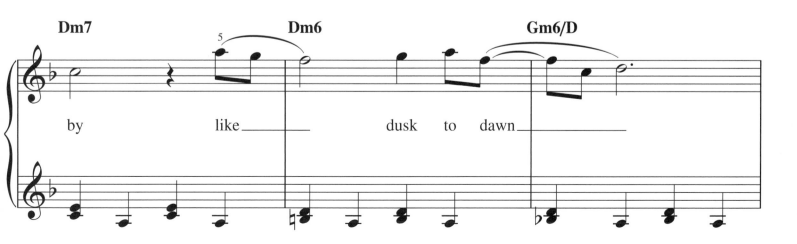

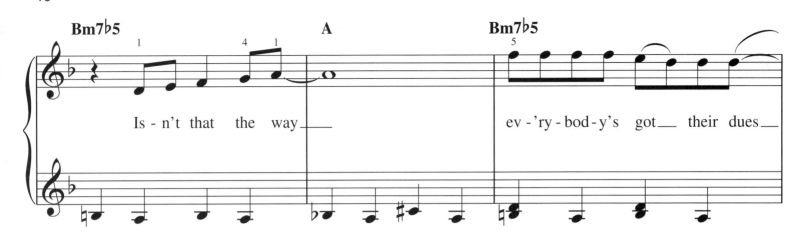

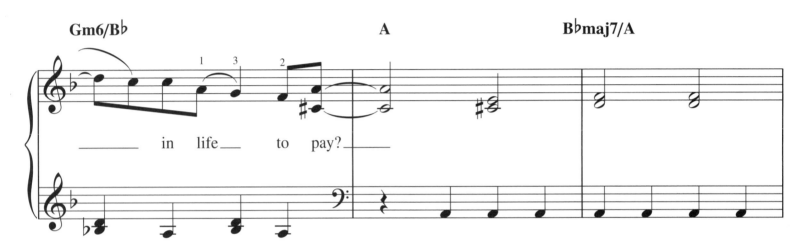

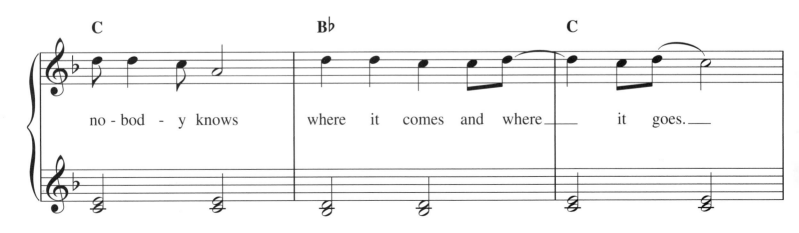

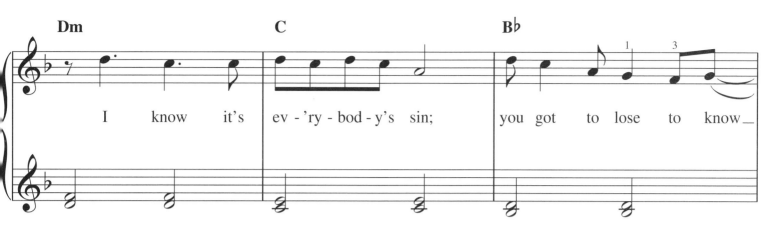

I know it's ev-'ry-bod-y's sin; you got to lose to know

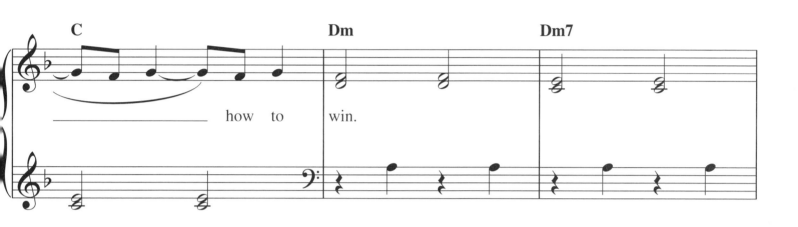

how to win.

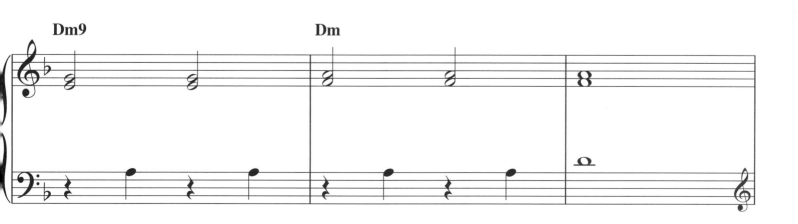

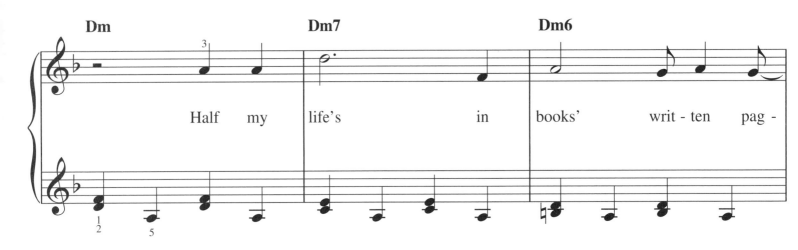

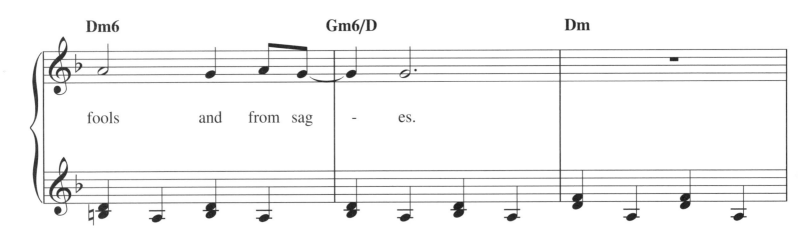

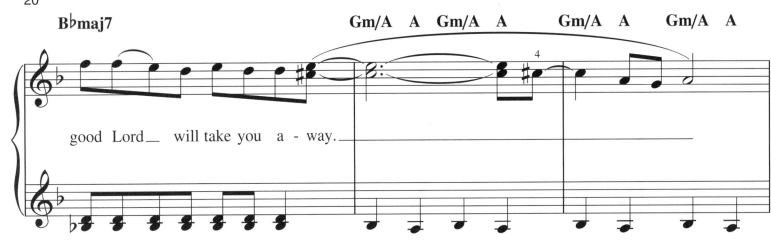

good Lord___ will take you a - way.___

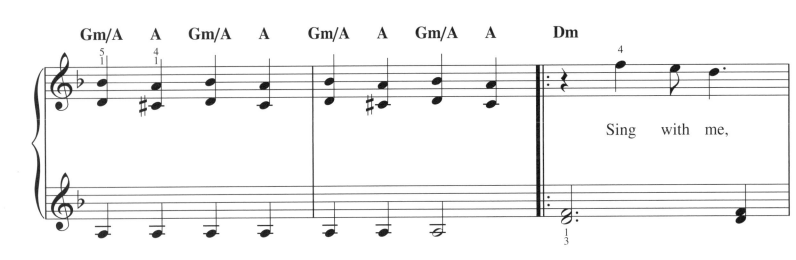

Sing with me,

sing for the years,___ sing for the laugh - ter 'n' sing___ for the tears.___

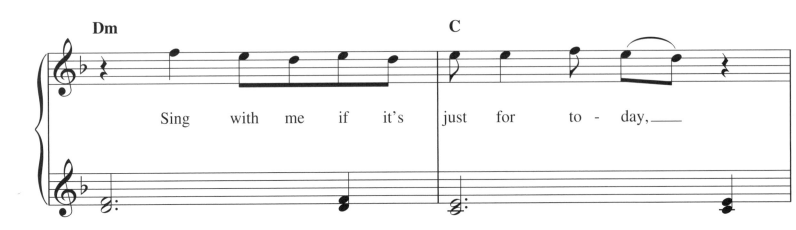

Sing with me if it's just for to - day,___

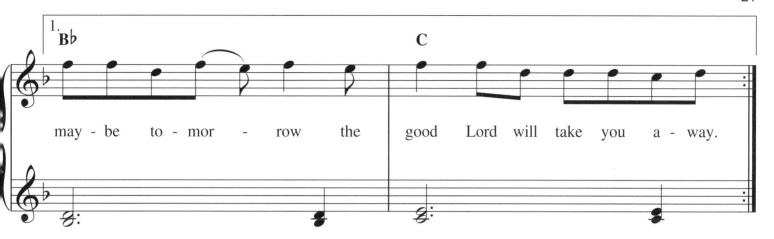

may - be to - mor - row the good Lord will take you a - way.

may - be to - mor - row the good Lord_ will take you a - way.

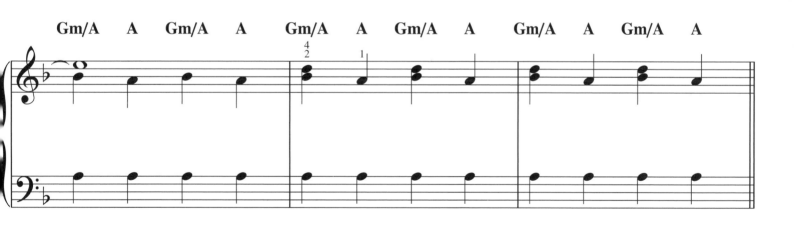

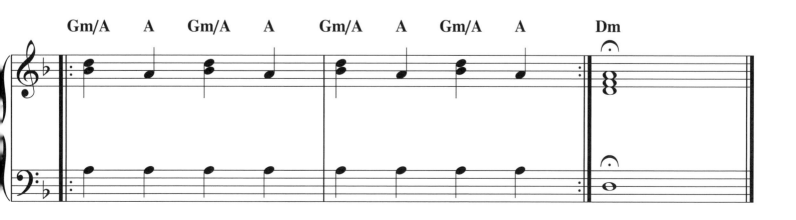

GIVE UP THE FUNK
(Tear the Roof Off the Sucker)

Words and Music by GEORGE CLINTON JR.,
WILLIAM "BOOTSY" COLLINS and JEROME BRAILEY

CODA

doo   doo   doo,   ow. _____   Ow,

we   want the funk,   give up the funk.   Ow,

we need the funk,   we've got to have the funk. Ow,   we've got to have the funk.

GIVES YOU HELL

Words and Music by TYSON RITTER
and NICK WHEELER

car? Did it ev - er get you far? You

nev - er seem so tense, love,
mor - row you'll be think - ing to your - self,

I've nev - er seen you fall so
"Where did __ it __ all go

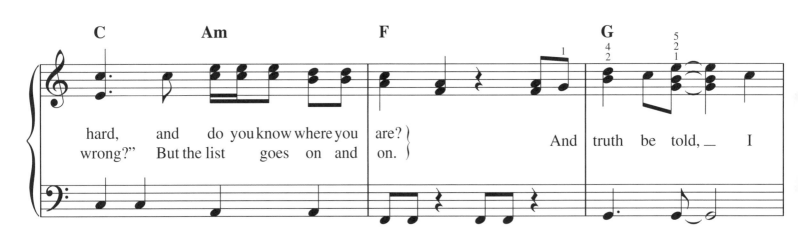

hard, and do you know where you are?
wrong?" But the list goes on and on.

And truth be told, __ I

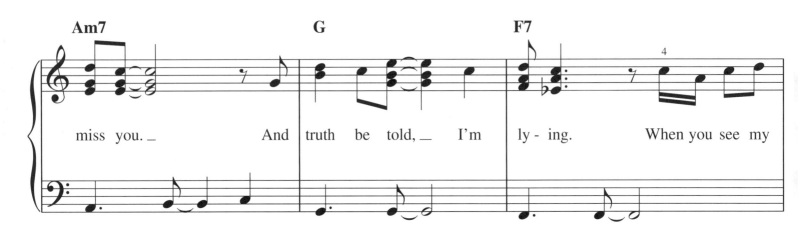

miss you. __ And truth be told, __ I'm ly - ing. When you see my

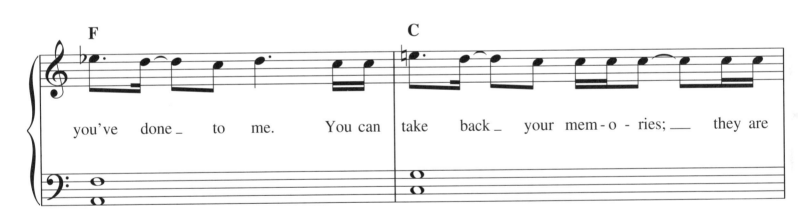

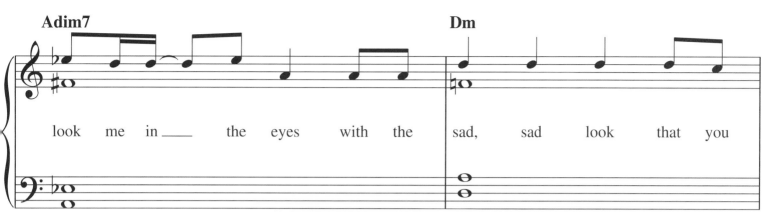

look me in ___ the eyes with the sad, sad look that you

wear so well. ___ When you see my

face, hope it gives you hell, hope it gives you hell. When you walk my

way, hope it gives you hell, hope it gives you hell. When you find a

man that's worth a damn and treats you well, then he's a

fool, you're just as well, hope it gives you hell. When you see my

face, hope it gives you hell, hope it gives you hell. When you walk my

way, hope it gives you hell, hope it gives you hell. When you hear this

song and you sing a - long, well, you'll nev - er tell. And you're the

fool, I'm just as well, hope it gives you hell. When you hear this

song I hope that it will give you hell. You can sing a -

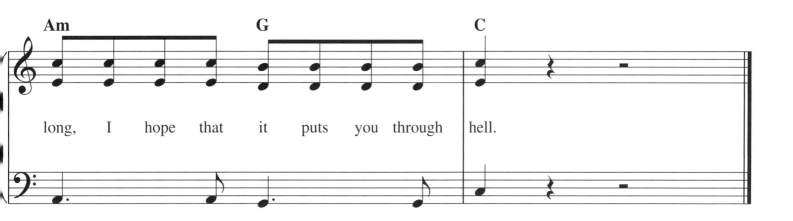

long, I hope that it puts you through hell.

HELLO

Words and Music by
LIONEL RICHIE

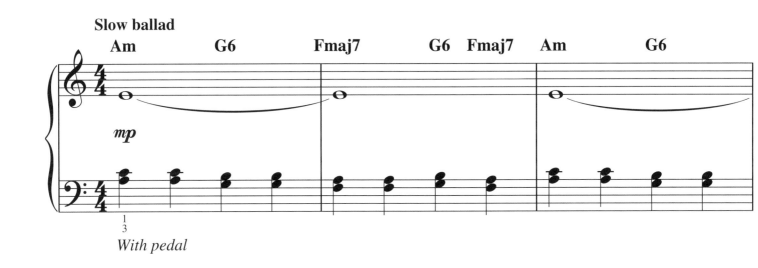

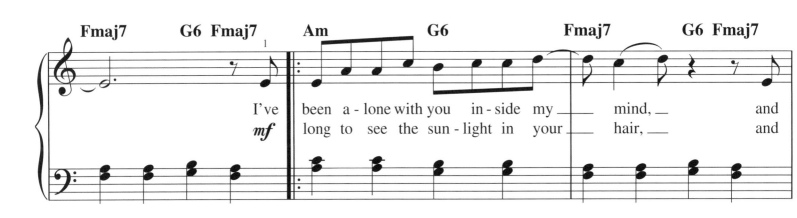

I've
long to see the sun-light in your

been a-lone with you in-side my
mind, and
hair, and

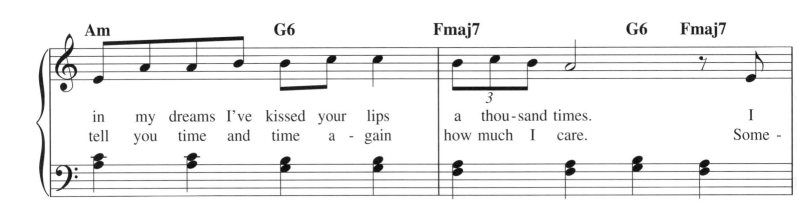

in my dreams I've kissed your lips a thou-sand times. I
tell you time and time a-gain how much I care. Some-

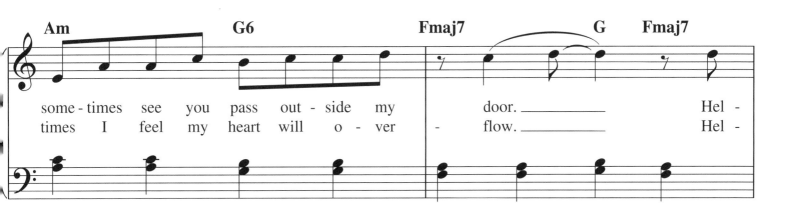

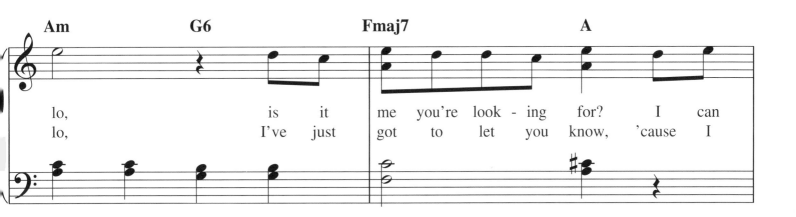

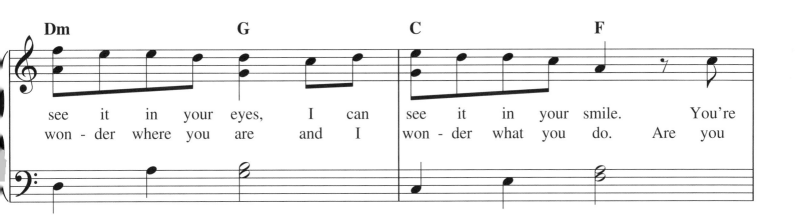

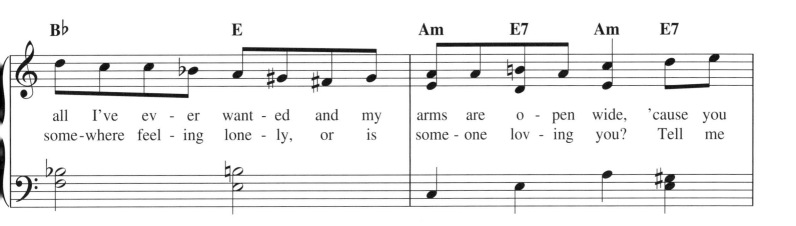

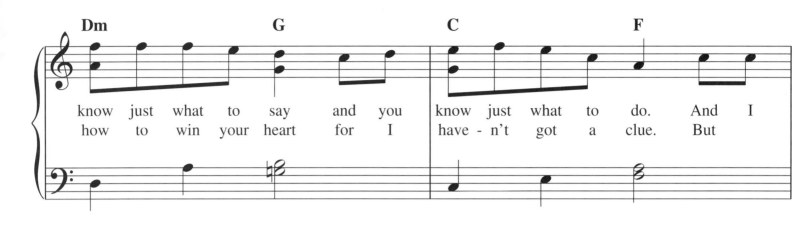

Dm ... **G** ... **C** ... **F**

know just what to say and you know just what to do. And I
how to win your heart for I have-n't got a clue. But

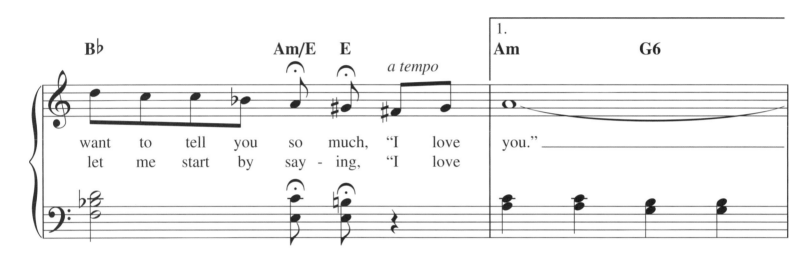

B♭ ... **Am/E** **E** ... *a tempo* ... | 1. **Am** ... **G6**

want to tell you so much, "I love you." _____
let me start by say - ing, "I love

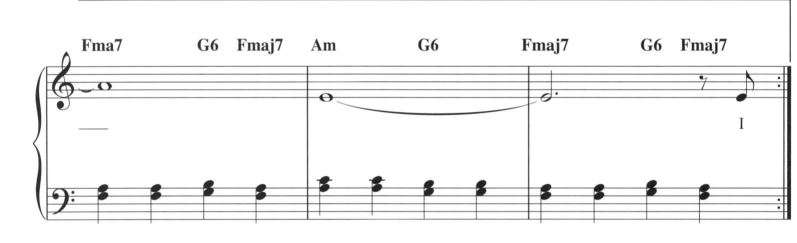

Fma7 ... **G6** **Fmaj7** ... **Am** ... **G6** ... **Fmaj7** ... **G6** **Fmaj7**

_____ I

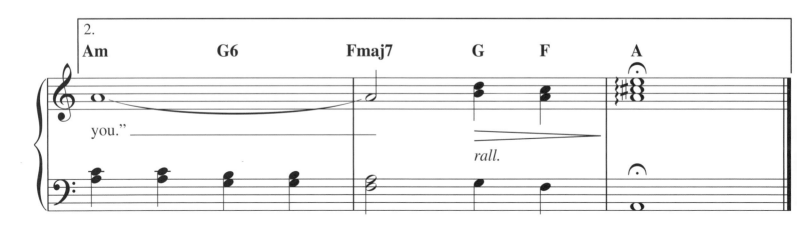

| 2. **Am** ... **G6** ... **Fmaj7** ... **G** **F** ... **A**

you." _____

rall.

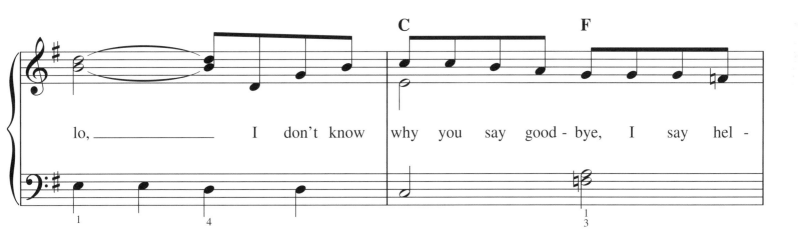

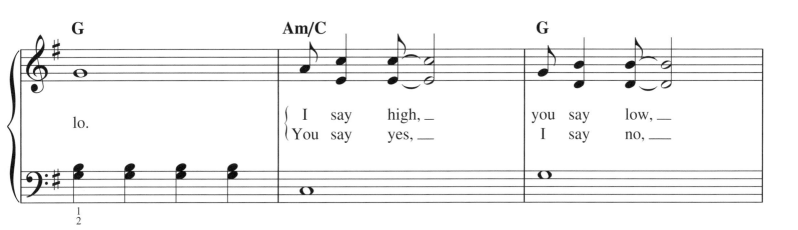

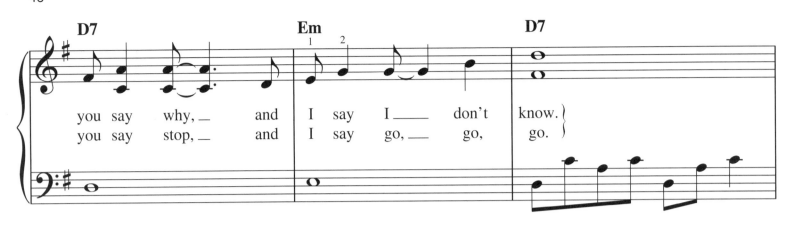

you say why, ___ and I say I ___ don't know.
you say stop, ___ and I say go, ___ go, go.

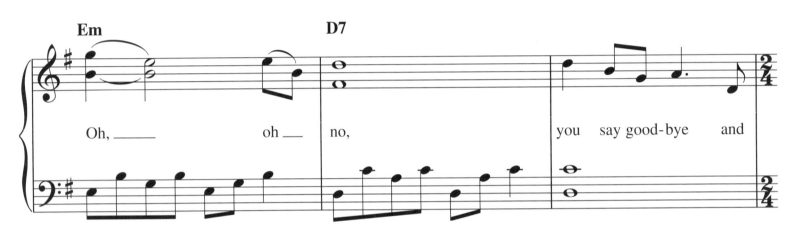

Oh, _____ oh ___ no, you say good-bye and

I say hel - lo. _____ Hel - lo, hel - lo, _____ I don't know

why you say good - bye, I say hel - lo. _____ Hel - lo, hel -

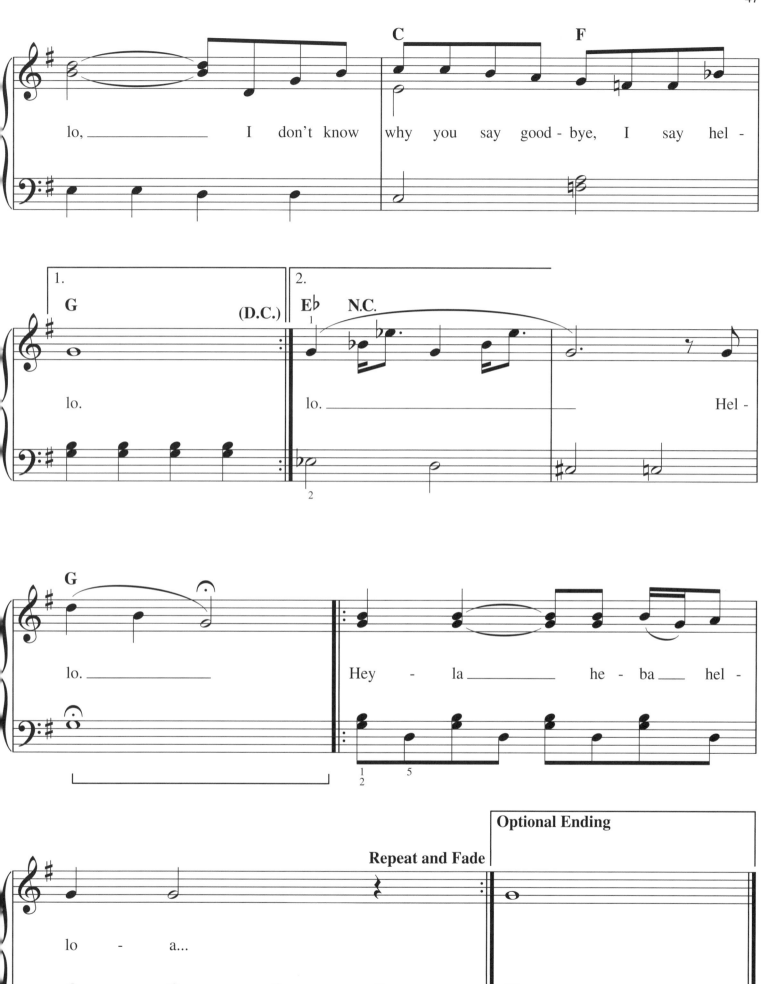

A HOUSE IS NOT A HOME

Lyric by HAL DAVID
Music by BURT BACHARACH

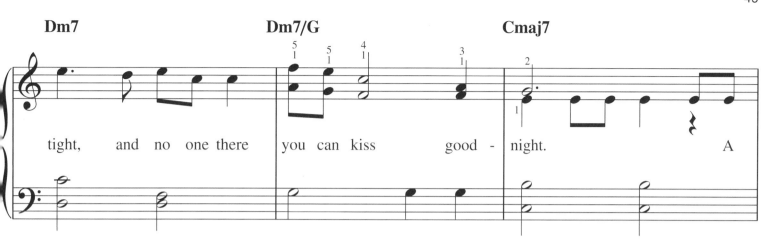

tight,   and   no   one there   you can kiss   good - night.   A

room   is   still   a   room _____   e - ven   when there's noth - ing

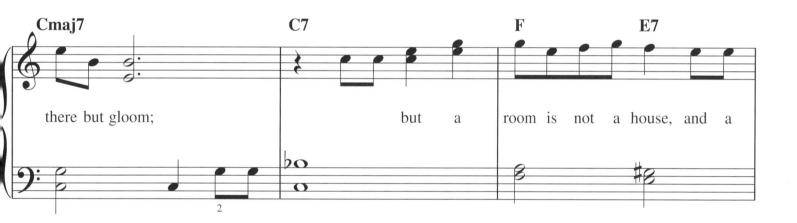

there but gloom;   but   a   room   is   not   a house, and a

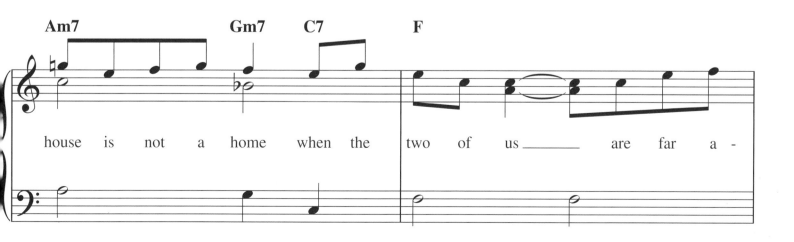

house   is   not   a   home   when the   two   of   us _____   are   far   a -

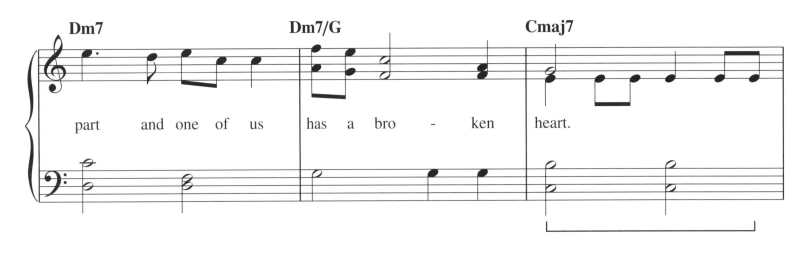

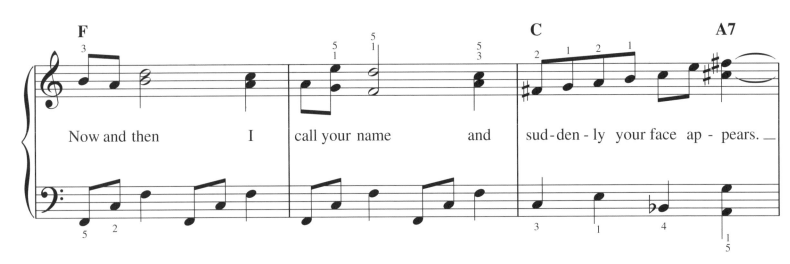

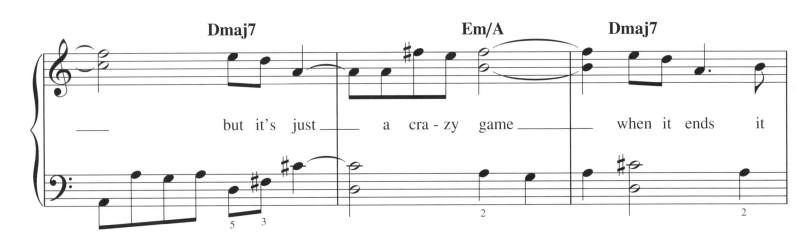

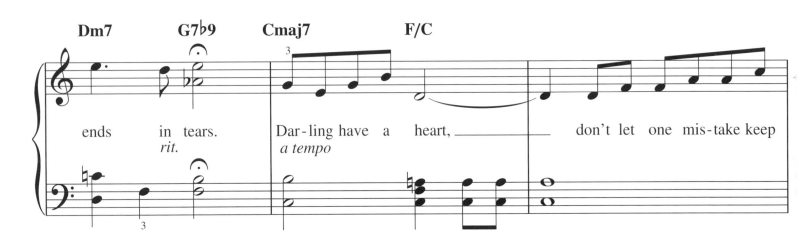

ONE

Lyrics by BONO and THE EDGE
Music by U2

C — **Am** — **F**

one love, — one life, — when it's one need
too late — to - night — to drag the past out in -
ask too much, — more than a lot? — You gave me noth-ing, now it's

C — **To Coda** — **1. Am**

in the night. — One love, — we get to share it.
to the light. — We're one, but we're
all I got. — We're one, but we're

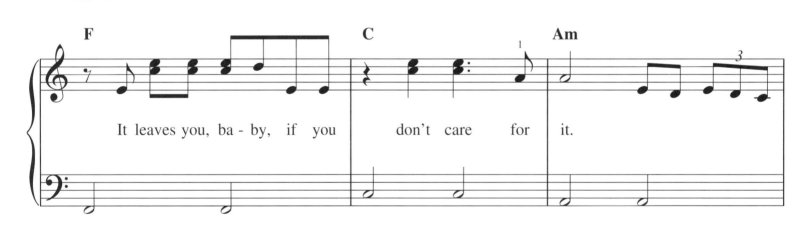

F — **C** — **Am**

It leaves you, ba - by, if you — don't care for it.

Dm — **F** — **G**

Love is a tem-ple. Love the high-er law. You ask me to en-ter, but

then you make me crawl. And I can't be hold-ing on to what you got

when all you got is hurt. One love, one blood,

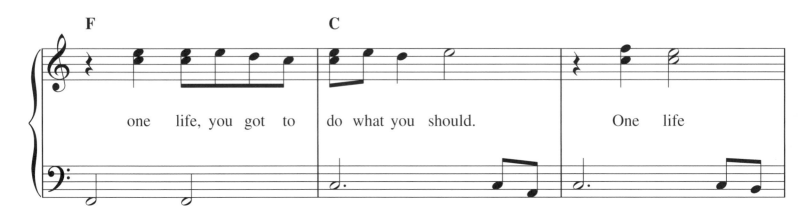

one life, you got to do what you should. One life

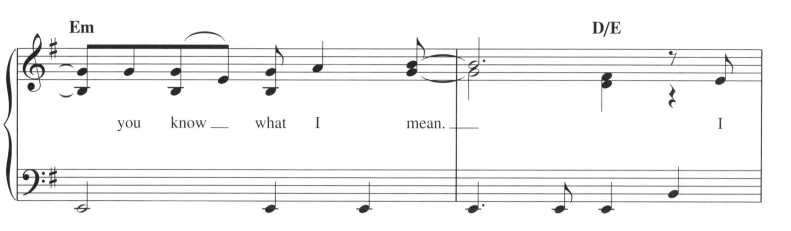

you know ___ what I mean. ___ I

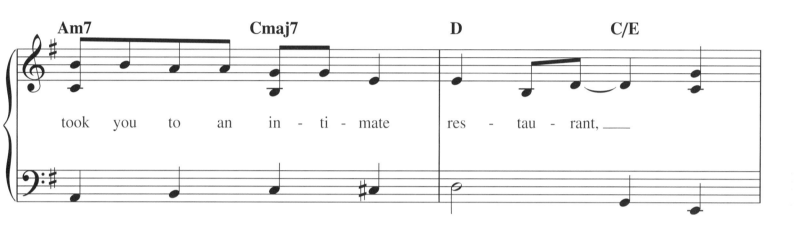

took you to an in - ti - mate res - tau - rant, ___

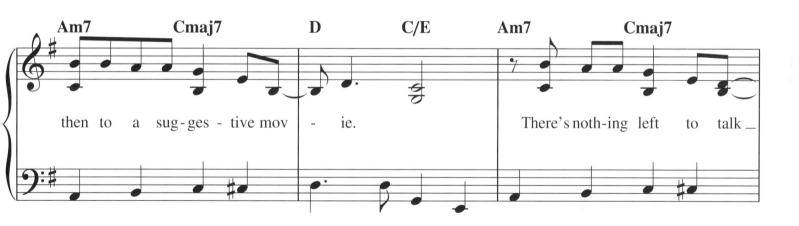

then to a sug - ges - tive mov - ie. There's noth-ing left to talk ___

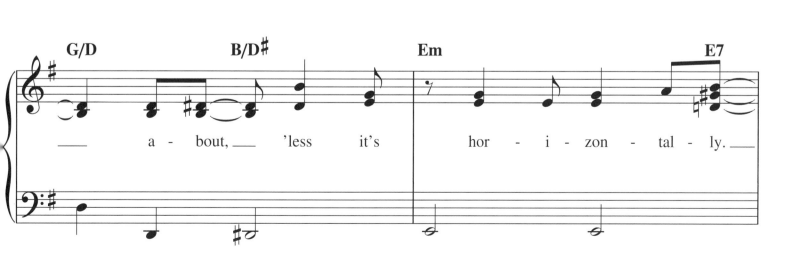

___ a - bout, ___ 'less it's hor - i - zon - tal - ly. ___

68

CODA

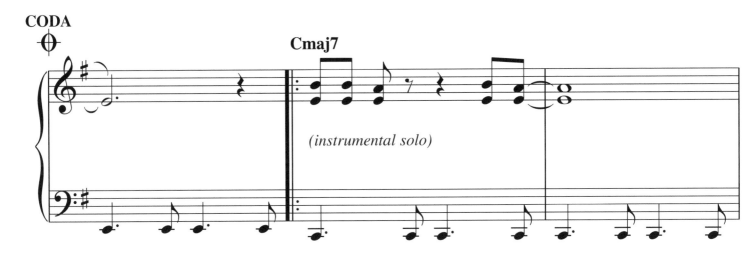

(instrumental solo)

Em

Let me hear your bod - y   talk. __

Repeat and Fade

Let me hear your bod - y   talk. _____

Additional Lyrics

2. I've been patient, I've been good,
   try'n to keep my hands on the table.
   It's gettin' hard, this holdin' back,
   you know what I mean.
   I'm sure you'll understand my point of view,
   we know each other mentally,
   You've gotta know that you're bringin' out
   the animal in me.
   Chorus

THE SAFETY DANCE

Words and Music by
IVAN DOROSCHUK

Moderately, with a beat

We can dance if we want to, we can leave your friends be-
We can go when we want to, the night is young and so am
(See additional lyrics)

hind. 'Cause your friends don't dance, and if they don't dance, well,
I. And we can dress real neat from our hats to our feet, and sur-

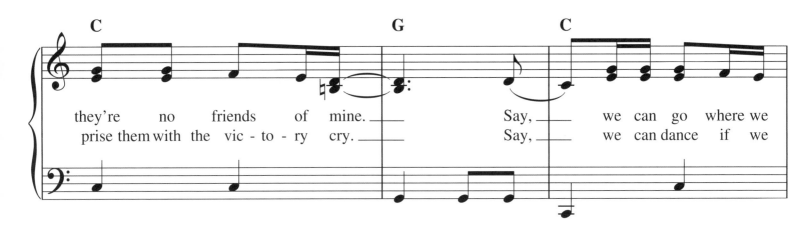

they're no friends of mine. ___ Say, ___ we can go where we
prise them with the vic - to - ry cry. ___ Say, ___ we can dance if we

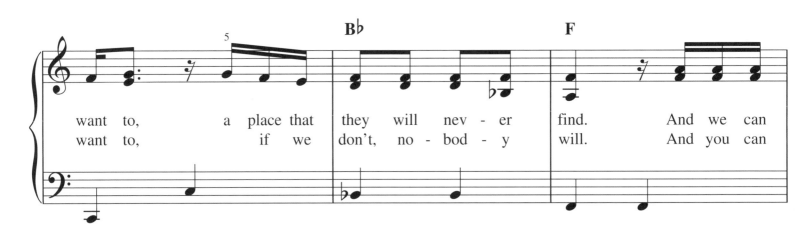

want to, a place that they will nev - er find. And we can
want to, if we don't, no - bod - y will. And you can

act like we come from out of this world, leave the real one far be - hind. ___
act real rude or to - tal - ly re - moved, and I can act like an im - be - cile. ___

1.

___ And we can dance.
___ Say,

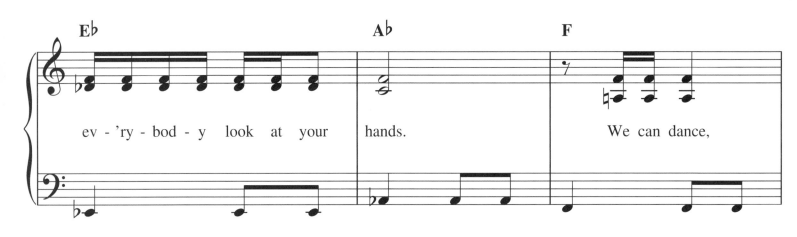

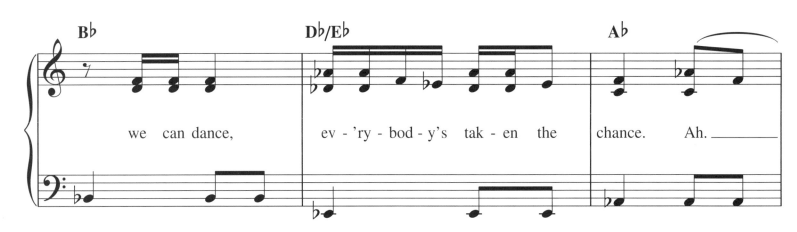

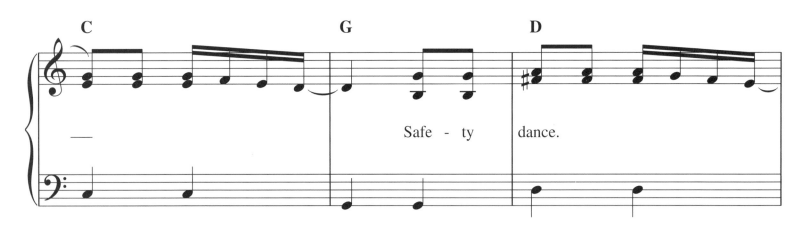

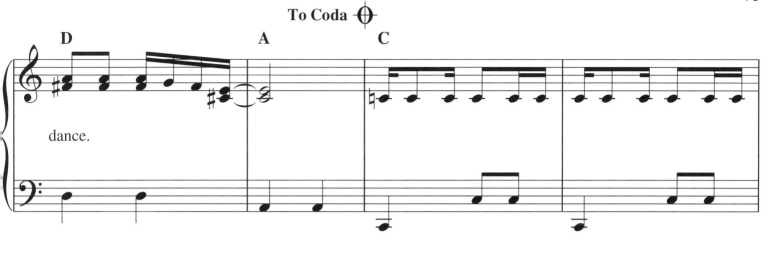

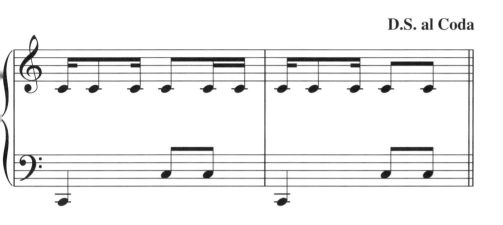
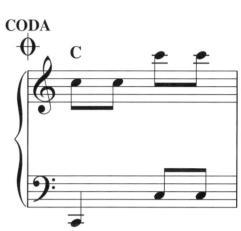

Additional Lyrics

We can dance if we want to,
We've got all your life and mine.
As long as we abuse it,
We're never gonna lose it,
And ev'rything will work out right.
Say, we can dance if we want to,
We can leave your friends behind.
'Cause your friends don't dance,
And if they don't dance,
Well, they're no friends of mine.

Say, we can dance...

TOTAL ECLIPSE OF THE HEART

Words and Music by
JIM STEINMAN

Moderately

Turn a - round.___ Ev -'ry now and then I get a lit - tle bit lone - ly and you're
Turn a - round.___ Ev -'ry now and then I get a lit - tle bit rest - less and I
Instrumental
Turn a - round.___ Ev -'ry now and then I know you'll nev - er be the boy you al - ways

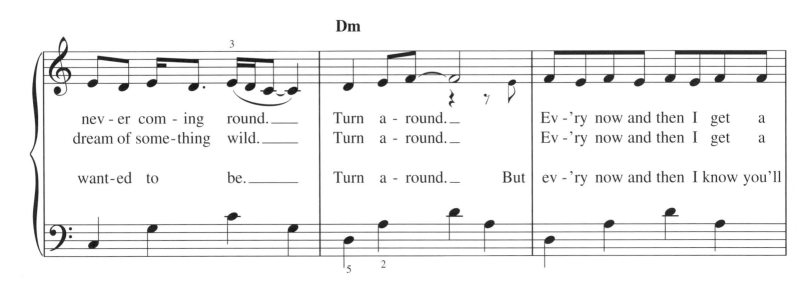

nev - er com - ing round.___ Turn a - round.___ Ev -'ry now and then I get a
dream of some - thing wild.___ Turn a - round.___ Ev -'ry now and then I get a
want - ed to be.___ Turn a - round.___ But ev -'ry now and then I know you'll

on-ly hold___ me tight,___ we'll be hold-ing on___ for-

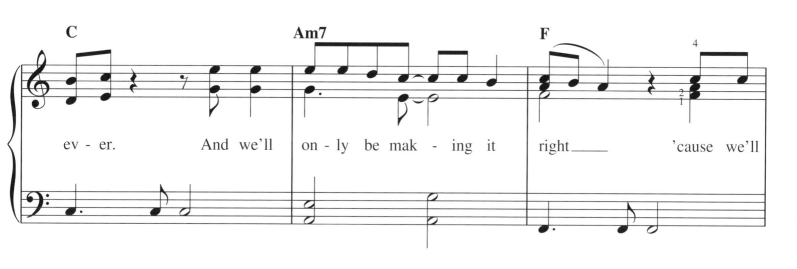

ev-er. And we'll on-ly be mak-ing it right___ 'cause we'll

nev-er be wrong___ to-geth-er we can take it to the end of the line.__ Your

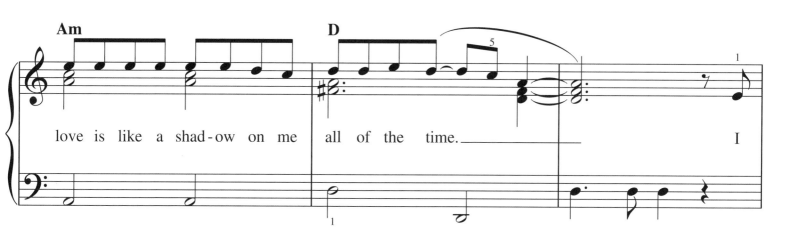

love is like a shad-ow on me all of the time._____ I

don't know what to do and I'm al - ways in the dark, __ we're liv - ing in a pow-der keg and

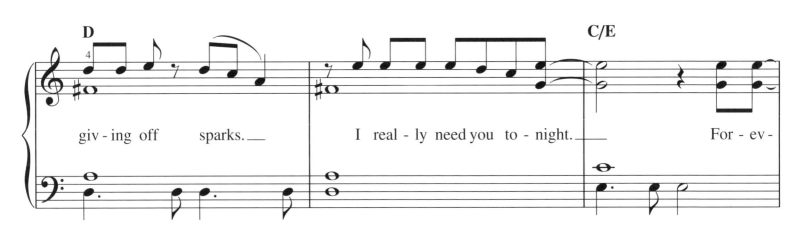

giv - ing off sparks. __ I real - ly need you to - night. __ For - ev-

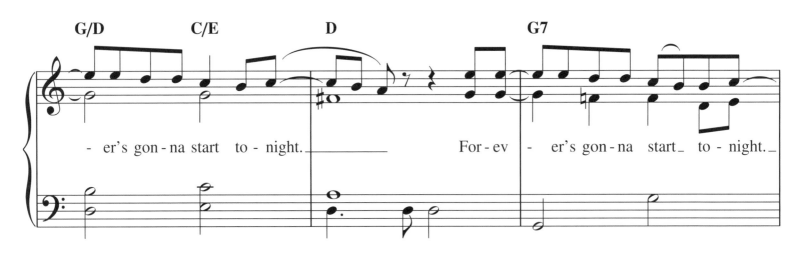

- er's gon - na start to - night. __ For - ev - er's gon - na start __ to - night. __

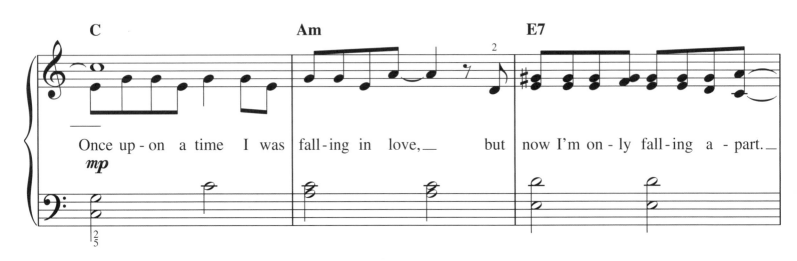

Once up - on a time I was fall - ing in love, __ but now I'm on - ly fall - ing a - part. __

mp

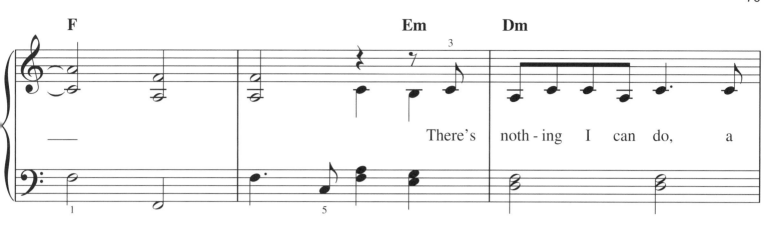

There's | noth-ing I can do, a

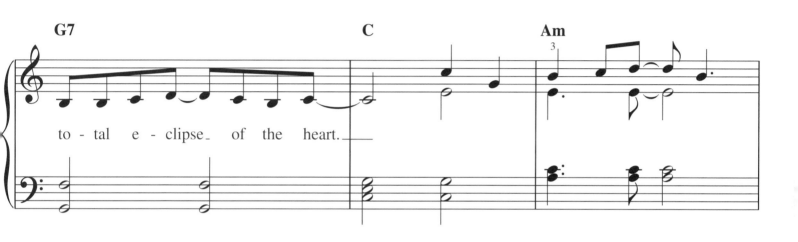

to - tal e - clipse_ of the heart.__

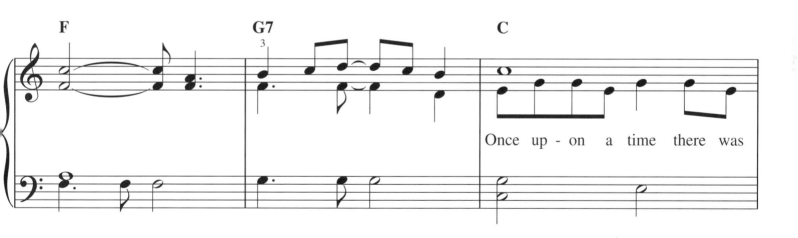

Once up-on a time there was

light in my life,__ but | now there's on - ly love in the dark.__

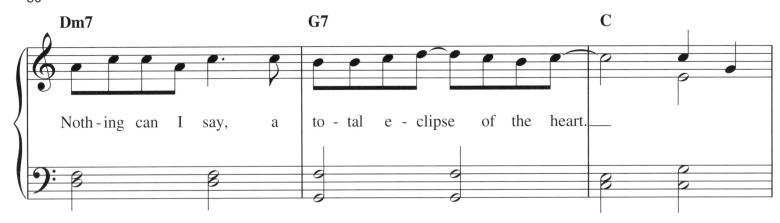

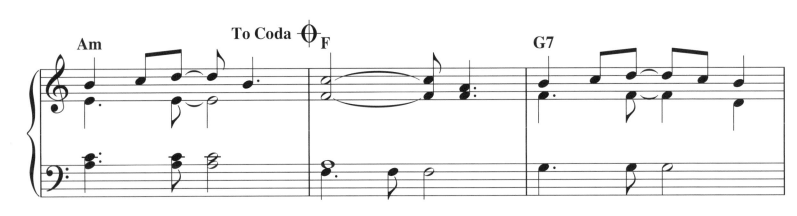

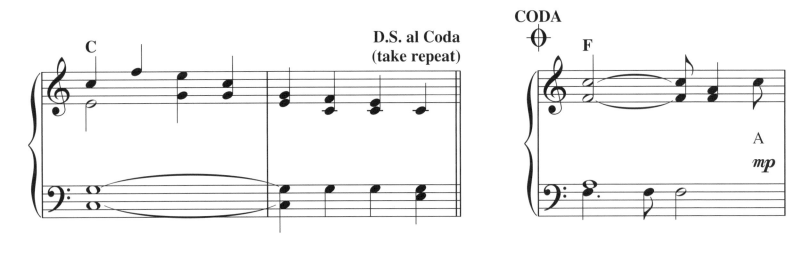